MA
WO
Pocketbook

By Will Thomas

Cartoons:
Phil Hailstone

POLICIES
Handbook
NATIONAL CURRICULUM
DfES
REGISTER
Mark Book

I ♥ SCH

Published by:

Teachers' Pocketbooks
Laurel House, Station Approach,
Alresford, Hampshire SO24 9JH, UK
Tel: +44 (0)1962 735573
Fax: +44 (0)1962 733637
E-mail: sales@teacherspocketbooks.co.uk
Website: www.teacherspocketbooks.co.uk

*Teachers' Pocketbooks is an imprint of
Management Pocketbooks Ltd.*

With thanks to Brin Best for his help in
launching the series.

This edition published 2005.
Reprinted 2007, 2010.

ISBN 978 1 903776 63 6
British Library Cataloguing-in-Publication
Data. A catalogue record for this book is
available from the British Library.

Design, typesetting and graphics by Efex Ltd.
Printed in UK

Contents

Introduction

I spent my early years in the teaching profession working too hard, playing too little and kidding myself I was having fun. You can't be resourceful, inspire and support others when you are not giving enough back to yourself.

Lights go on and off in your life. In 1998 two very bright lights faded and went out in one year. Two much-loved colleagues very sadly died within a few months of one another. When they died it set me thinking about how much every moment matters. School culture is a wonderfully warm and enveloping blanket, but it can sometimes smother you: when you are no longer aware of the hours you are actually putting in; when you are no longer aware of the cost to those you love most.

It **really is possible** to perform well at work and enjoy a healthy, happy rounded life. In fact your performance will improve precisely because you are happier, healthier and more rounded.

Introduction

Teaching is an extremely challenging profession, but there are ways you can
make it easier. To be the best we can be to our students, our school, our families,
friends and ourselves involves balance. To get this you will need to be willing to:

- Be really honest with yourself
- Commit to removing sources of stress from your life, including thinking differently
- Try new (and old) ways of working
- Challenge some of the limiting thoughts and ideas that you have created
  in the past
- Make reading this book, and the actions you take from it, a turning point for you

By shifting your approach and thinking, you will create a more effective
work-life balance. A few small changes can add up to big benefits over the mid-
and long-term.

Introduction

This book is for anyone who ever feels they could be using time better, working more effectively and enjoying life more. It is aimed at teachers, student teachers, education leaders and other education professionals who would like to understand the processes of stress, further enhance their abilities to manage it, and get more balance and fulfilment in their lives.

The following pages give you practical advice that will allow you to do the best for your students and be an even better teacher and leader. If you are **new** to the profession, how you set your boundaries and systems of working will shape your enjoyment of the coming years; if you are an **established** teacher, remember that appropriate change keeps us and our colleagues fresh and vital. Approaches you tried in the past that didn't work as well then may actually be the right next step for you now.

Introduction

All of the techniques and suggestions I make here have been used either by me or by other teachers in schools and colleges. As with any set of advice, you have the freedom to choose what to try. The self-evaluation at the end of the book provides a framework for examining your current approaches to managing workload.

It is nonsense to separate your work and your personal life when it comes to managing workload; your life is your whole life. So I would invite you to consider the bigger picture and I hope in many ways this book may even change your life...are you working to live or living to work?

Notes

Work-Life Balance ◀

 Winning Attitudes

 Great Habits

 Taming Time

 Looking After Yourself

 Self-evaluation Framework

Work-Life Balance

What is it costing you?

The statistics:

- In 2002, statistically speaking, each teacher in the maintained sector had an average of 5.5 days off sick in a school year
- 57% of teachers took time off and the average number of days for this group was close to 10
- Stress-related illness is the fourth <u>official</u> reason for teachers taking time off sick
- Headteachers in one survey, reported in the TES in 2004, felt that more than 50% of staff absence in their school was due to stress

Anyone who has spent time at the chalk face knows that the job can be tremendously taxing. Making hundreds of decisions and managing thousands of variables in each classroom each day can take its toll. Stress may be one of the most significant reasons for staff absence, and perhaps underlies some of the physical symptoms that cause teachers to take time off.

What is work-life balance?

Work-life balance is about adjusting your working patterns so that you find a rhythm which combines work with other responsibilities and aspirations.

The result of being out of balance with your workload is that negative stress can occur. This can lead to physical, mental and emotional ill health, not to mention lowered performance, expectation and achievement in all aspects of your life.

The good news

The government has already committed to reducing teacher workload with its **school workforce remodelling** agenda.

Remodelling is about giving teachers more time, extra support and renewed leadership. This is essential if they are to go on improving standards in schools. By restructuring the teaching profession and reforming the school workforce, we can reduce teacher workload, raise standards, increase job satisfaction and improve the status of the profession. DfES

But let's be really clear:
In some schools workforce reform has had a really positive impact on teacher work-life balance. In others less so. Whilst government and school leadership can make a difference to your workload, they are likely to play a small part in relation to the day-to-day management of your portfolio. It is personal organisation, effective habits of mind and determination to make positive changes that will have the most impact on your work-life balance.

If you want them to, **the changes can begin right now**.

Managing workload – 5 steps

There are five key steps to bringing greater balance and managing your workload more effectively:

1. **Evaluate now** – evaluate the current position and plan regular review slots, celebrate your successes, plan your next steps.
2. **Choose your future** – identify in detail what kind of balance you would like.
3. **Identify habits** – identify the habits which waste time and energy, and replace with winning approaches.
4. **Plan your strategy** –identify the strategies that will move you towards the future you wish for (use this book and other resources to support you).
5. **Act NOW** – take action NOW to start that process of change.

Evaluating your life

Evaluation is the first step towards further improving your workload management and to bringing greater balance to your life. It is also an essential, on-going process of review.

When we are working hard we can sometimes lose sight of the truth of our current situation. The following pages outline an activity you can use to enable you to get an overview of the current position with your workload.

What to do now:
- Create a space of 20 minutes to carry out this review process
- Work through the work-life balance focus tool activity that follows

WARNING: Carrying out this activity can lead to seriously positive improvements in your work-life balance!

The work-life focus tool

Satisfaction level is a useful starting point for exploring balance.
This activity will help you determine your current level of satisfaction with your life.

By scoring on a scale of 1 to 10 how satisfied you are with each area of your life, you can begin to see where there is a need for balancing effort. In the grid below there is an example of one person's satisfaction profile. When you do yours on the grid overleaf, choose your own column headings so they fit your situation.

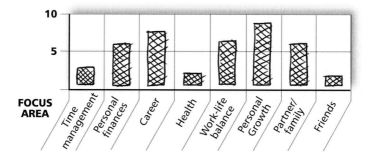

Satisfaction profile

1. Use the grid below to divide your life into up to eight key areas. Choose the areas yourself to reflect all aspects of your life.
2. Next, score each section from 1 to 10 based on your level of satisfaction with each area. (10 is completely satisfied, 1 is very unsatisfied)

Once you have completed the grid, continue onto the next page to explore what you found

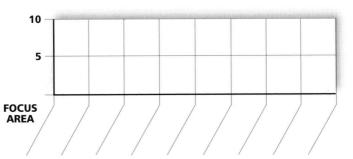

A downloadable/printable version of this tool is available at
http://visionforlearning.co.uk/mlpbresources

Analysing your satisfaction

Now ask yourself the following questions:

- Where are you most satisfied?
- Where are you least satisfied?
- What patterns, if any, do you notice?
- Is there a particular area of dissatisfaction that you would like to enhance?
- Based on this activity what is in balance and what is out of balance in your life right now?
- If you could change one thing in your life right now, what might it be?
- What are the key things you have learned from this activity?

Some great news

The results of the work-life balance tool may well have helped you identify some areas of your life that need attention. There may be patterns emerging or connections that you see now, but didn't see before the exercise. The activity may simply have confirmed earlier thoughts.

The important thing now is to look at the preferred future you desire and to take steps to create more of what you want in terms of satisfaction.

THE GOOD NEWS IS…..you can make significant improvements to your work-life balance.

If you are satisfied, congratulations. You may still find the ideas in this book useful to further cut your workload and enhance balance.

Something to think about

Friends, family, work and futures
We juggle many balls each day: our friends, our family, our professional responsibilities and our aspirations for the future.

Up in the air the balls go, over and down. Some we can throw really high and still catch, others we keep close to us. Every so often we drop balls and they hit the ground. Some balls are the ones made of high density rubber and they spring back high in the air and back into our hands. Others drop with a dull thud and stay there until, at some point, we pick them up. No harm done. Some balls, however, are made of crystal and as they fall and hit the ground they shatter.

- Which balls are the rubber ones in your life?
- Which are the ones that hang around until you pick them up again?
- Which balls are the crystals, the gems, that once dropped are never the same again?

" With their dying breath, a teacher never says, 'I wish I'd spent more time with my school work.' "

The future

If you want more balance, get in touch with what it is like to already have it

Having gained more insight into your work-life balance you can now decide how to move things forward. This involves considering your preferred future.

For some people, asking questions about the future is exciting, for others it can be unnerving. Some of us prefer to let fate take its course, but the trouble with this is it usually means someone else is deciding our fate.

Researchers in the field of human motivation and development have shown that deciding on the future you would prefer, and becoming really sure about what you want, primes your subconscious mind to look for the opportunities and resources around you which will help you achieve this preferred future. Our minds filter information which is important to us. What we pay attention to is largely a matter of what our subconscious mind is attuned to.

Preferred futures

It's time to create your preferred future so you know what you are working towards. This exercise can seem a little strange, but stick with it.

Step 1.
Decide what you would prefer your work-life balance to be like. Be specific.

- What will it look like/sound like/feel like when you have this?

- What positive things will others be saying/noticing/doing?

- What exactly will you have and be when you have achieved this balance?

Preferred futures

Step 2.
Go ahead into the future (you choose how far, eg six months, one year, three years, etc) to a time when you already have this work-life balance

- What does it look like/sound like/feel like now that you have it?

- What exactly do you have in the future that shows you have achieved this balance? How are you different as a person now that you have it?

With a preferred future developed in your mind, it's time to consider the goals you will need to set to achieve this.

The power of goals

A research project began at Yale University in America in the 1950's. Graduates were surveyed at the start of the project and again 20 years later. It found that, financially, 3% of the graduates were worth more than the remaining 97% and that they enjoyed better health and relationships. On analysis, it was found that the key difference between the 3% and the 97% was the 3% had set and actually written down detailed goals in the 1950's.

As a backlash to the target-centred culture in schools it can be tempting to dismiss the concept of setting and writing down personal goals. However, when you focus on specific goals, you tune yourself into noticing even more of the opportunities around you to achieve them.

To bring your work-life balance hopes to fruition turn your preferred future into clear written goals.

Goal-setting

'Each year, between Christmas and New Year, I find a quiet hour to reflect. I think about what I have achieved over the past year and allow myself to take credit for the success. I move on to consider all the things I have learned and then I ask myself what I would like to achieve in the coming year. I allow myself the 'freedom of anything'; that means I just throw around ideas and no matter how mad they seem I write them down. Often the maddest ideas give me other thoughts and I get into a very creative process. Once I have all of those down on paper I identify the goals from my thoughts and refine those on paper. Almost immediately I can feel myself looking for ways to achieve those goals, giving them a profile in my mind. From that point it becomes easier to achieve, to feel fulfilled and to make things happen.'

**Caroline, Primary School Teacher,
Surrey**

SMART goals

When you translate your preferred future into a clear written goal, make it: **SMART**:

S pecific: State the goal in terms of what you have when it's achieved, eg *'I am... I have...'*

M easurable: Be clear about how you will measure the outcome, ie how will you know you have achieved your goal?

A chievable: Choose a goal which can be achieved, eg *'I am under 35 swimming champion'* (and you're now 33)

R ealistic: Choose a goal which feels realistic, eg *'I am headteacher of this school next term'* (You are currently acting head)

T imed: Place a timescale on it – set a date/time

An example:

I am working no more than XX hours per term week and XX hours of my holiday time by 21st November 200X. I know this from auditing the hours I work once per half term and comparing with target hours. I am spending XX hours per school week relaxing with my family.

Your key to success

Now you know how to set specific goals you need to do the following:

- Go back to your work-life focus tool
- **For each area** you identified in the tool, work out the SMART goals you need to set for the **next 12 months** and set them. (For some people, thinking further ahead is of great help and you may wish to think of your three- or five-year goals in planning the next 12 months)
- For each goal consider what it will look/feel/sound like when you have achieved it
- Write every goal down using the SMART format
- What isn't in the work-life balancing tool that needs to be? Add it and work out the goals

These goals are your key to success.

From now on look at them and read them every day. By keeping them at the forefront of your mind you will notice the opportunities that are already around you to achieve them.

Parkinson's law

Now that you have begun to consider where you are currently with work-life balance, you can move towards choosing the future you would prefer. Consider this:

Parkinson's Law: *Work expands to fill the time you make available to it*

This means that the longer you are prepared to push the boundaries of work into the rest of your life, the more work will spill into your personal time.

An essential goal for anyone serious about reining in their hours at work is to create and use a **working envelope**.

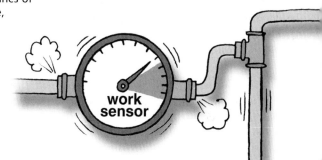

The working envelope

The DfEE (CIPD) work-life balance survey 2000 found that of those workers who worked more than 48 hours per week:

- 70% of long-hours workers were too tired to hold a conversation
- 43% of partners of long-hours workers were 'fed up' with having to shoulder the domestic burdens
- 29% of partners of long-hours workers felt that the long hours had 'a quite or very negative effect' on their partner's relationship with their children
- 56% of long-hours workers said they had dedicated too much of their time to their work
- In more than a third of cases children reported that they didn't see enough of their long-hours worker parent

The working envelope offers an aproach to balancing work with the rest of your life.

Envelope case study

Yorkshire Teacher and Curriculum Manager:

'My working envelope consists of getting in early and working until 5.30pm. That is it. I get in early and leave late, and only rarely take work home. I assume I will lose my free time and so when I get it, it is a real bonus. After school on a Thursday is always planning for the following week and after school on a Monday is always longer term planning for the coming half term. I spend my evenings with my family, on household chores and doing things I enjoy. This leaves me refreshed and ready for the next day. Most of the marking and feedback I provide goes on in class. I do the job well, because I know when to switch on and when to switch off. To me, being fresh and energetic for the students each day is what makes teaching such a rewarding career.'

Everyone is different and it may suit your circumstances to work in other ways, but this teacher has found great benefit in creating a tight working pattern that separates home and work.

Making the envelope

❓ *How much time do you want to spend each week working?*

This is a highly individual matter and depends on so many parameters in your life. You may have some unrealistic expectations! It is important to keep in mind that teaching is a profession which makes demands of you beyond the confines of your contact time with pupils. You need to feel you have this time under control if you are to balance your life.

It may be important for you to set challenging targets for reducing your working envelope. It is vital, however, that you build in realistic timescales for reducing workload.

If your work is currently overwhelming you, there may be a number of key areas to consider.

These matters may take some time to address, so be kind to yourself and give yourself reasonable timescales for change. The result of setting unreasonable demands is often disappointment and consequently loss of resilience.

Defining your envelope

1. Be clear about how much time you are contractually expected to work over a year.

2. How many hours do you typically work per week? (include before work, after work, at home, at weekends and in the holidays).

3. Total up the hours you spend above this contractual obligation.

4. Consider how much time you are *really* happy to put in each week.

5. Decide on a working envelope for a week.

6. Plot the time you will spend working on the grid overleaf.

Working envelope grid

Time	Monday	Tuesday	Wednesday	Thursday	Friday	Saturday	Sunday
6:00							
7:00							
8:00							
9:00							
10:00							
11:00							
12:00							
13:00							
14:00							
15:00							
16:00							
17:00							
18:00							
19:00							
20:00							
21:00							
22:00							

Consider this over a few days and tweak until you are content with it. Now sign a contract with yourself here. This is my working envelope: _____

The longer view

Many teachers who use the working envelope principle to manage their workload say it works for them.

The envelope is an excellent checker of time spent on work. It is important to treat it as a flexible tool and not as an absolute boundary. Inevitably, demands rise and fall, and occasionally there are unplanned issues which mean you need to stretch your envelope. There are also more demanding times of the year than others. All this must be borne in mind.

To slavishly stick to the envelope can create resentment and a range of unhelpful emotions. Being flexible is good. Being a walk-over is not good. So decide what you will accept. If you absolutely have to stretch your envelope one week, take back that time in the following week. Taking a balanced view of the envelope over a month is a helpful approach.

The grid opposite is available to download from the 'workload' area of http://visionforlearning.co.uk/mlpbresources

Balancing

We have met the term 'work-life balance' many times so far in this book. In fact an important concept is that: **_'We don't achieve balance but achieve balancing'_**

Many of us try and fail to juggle our priorities because when we achieve a success we allow ourselves to give up the strategies that got us there. The moment of balance is lost. We quickly fall back to a position of imbalance.

When we commit to making a difference to our lives, then we commit to work-life balancing. This involves setting very specific work-life balance goals and cultivating the behaviours that bring personal and professional effectiveness. There is no endpoint; it is ongoing actions which keep us balancing over time.

The next two sections of the book look at what gets in the way of achieving balancing and what we can do to gain and maintain work-life balance.

Work-Life
Balance

 Winning
Attitudes ◀

 Great
Habits

 Taming
Time

 Looking
After Yourself

 Self-evaluation
Framework

Winning
Attitudes

What gets in the way of balance?

There are five behaviours that get in the way of balancing:

- **Inappropriate prioritisation** – doing things in the wrong order of importance or doing some things at all
- **Procrastination** – avoidance behaviour that puts work off
- **Failure to delegate** – the 'If you want it done properly do it yourself' attitude
- **Limiting beliefs** – *'I can't…..because….'*
- **Interaction behaviours** – approaches to interacting with others which can hold you back

By exploring each of these you can work out which are holding you back from balance and what you can do to overcome them.

Inappropriate prioritisation

Not everything that comes into our lives is a priority. When we wrongly prioritise some things over others, we can unbalance ourselves.

If we **fail to prioritise** what we do, we become **reactive** rather than **proactive** and sometimes the trivial overrides the really important.

Keeping a log each day for a week of how you use your time can help to show patterns of inappropriate prioritisation. Though it initially takes time to do, it will reveal fascinating information that will help you improve your effectiveness.

Prioritising – strategies

A simple and very effective way to manage priorities is the URGENT–IMPORTANT grid. You can use the grid to identify the nature of a task.

Urgent and Important (UI)	**Non-Urgent but Important (NUI)**
Crisis management	Communication
Problems	Building teams
Some behaviour management issues	Planning ahead
	Anticipating issues and preparing
	Learning and preparing to enhance it
	Rest and recuperation
	Providing feedback to learners
Urgent but Not Important (UNI)	**Non-Urgent and Not Important (NUNI)**
Some interruptions	Quite a lot of email and snail mail
Some email/snail mail	Low level paperwork
Some other people's priorities	Bemoaning the teacher's lot
	Timewasters

Get into the habit of considering the urgency and importance of each task. If it isn't a UI or a NUI, then lower it in your priorities, or strike it out altogether.

Procrastination

Procrastination = avoidance behaviour that puts work off

We can put off doing tasks for a number of reasons:

- There are emotional difficulties attached to a task
- The task is large or complex, and we have not considered the steps involved
- The task involves interacting with someone we fear, or see as difficult to work with
- The job is uninspiring, requires a low level of skill, or does not seem to have a direct impact on improving learning

Procrastination – strategies

*'Tackle **first** the thing on your task list you most want to avoid!'*

- **Big or complex jobs** – spend some time breaking these into a series of smaller tasks, and plan when you will do each sub-task (eg: planning a set of lessons for a new syllabus)

- **High level cognitively challenging tasks** – do these when you have your highest energy levels in the day – avoid late afternoon (eg: understanding complex concepts and deciding how to teach them)

- **Low level, repetitive tasks** – work on these when you have low levels of energy. This can actually make such tasks more rewarding (eg: simple marking or making resources)

- **Emotionally challenging tasks** – predict the likely challenges and plan a range of assertive ways to deal with them. Ask others to help you think it through (eg: planning how to deal with the behaviour of a challenging student)

Procrastination – strategies

- **Above all, get started**. Do something, anything to get the ball rolling when you recognise yourself procrastinating (eg clear your desk of everything except one simple task and do it there and then)

- **Manage the complaining culture**. There can be in schools a culture of complaining about how bad things are. At a low level this can serve to acknowledge the strains of teaching, but if allowed to be the focus of interaction with others, it can lock you into a negative thinking cycle (page 47). Acknowledge the difficulties, then move on. (Eg: choose carefully who to spend time with during lunches and breaks, shift negative conversations to positive with a focus on humorous or successful events)

If you have a persistent problem with procrastination, the services of a life coach can be useful to help you break the patterns of behaviour that lead to it. Look for a coach who uses NLP coaching techniques.

Failure to delegate

The 'If you want it done properly do it yourself' attitude is the perfect way to destroy your work-life balance!

Most teachers and leaders in schools have the possibility of delegating some aspects of their work to others. There may even be genuinely appropriate roles for students to perform that help you and help them to develop new skills.

There are a number of reasons why teachers don't delegate tasks. Here are some:

- They think people won't do it the way they want it done
- They feel they will lose control
- They are uncertain about the ability of others to meet deadlines
- They really enjoy the fine details of a job
- They believe there's no one to delegate to
- They are uncomfortable about asking others to do things they consider to be their responsibility
- It takes time to set up delegation; they think it's easier to do it themselves

Delegating – strategies

Handled properly, delegation can save you considerable time and lets you focus on the high-importance tasks on your list. If you lead people in your school, you need to develop your ability to delegate. Over time you enhance the skills of others and gradually free up more of your time. Delegation can be a long-term solution to pressure.

'I delegate the job of organising teams for house sports events in my tutor group. I identify a small team of people to carry out the task and brief them carefully on the outcome and we discuss the approaches they might take. I coach the ideas from them. It works well: they negotiate and this leaves me free to get on with other things like following up absence and supporting individuals. As student confidence has grown I have steadily delegated more and more in my tutor group. Organising and leading aspects of the personal and social education lessons we have together has developed student social skills in its own right, alongside freeing me up.'

Linda,
Teacher and Form Tutor, Devon

Delegating – strategies

 Do:

- Choose tasks to delegate which **free you** to do planning
- **Be clear** about outcomes, deadlines and budgets
- Select people you believe have the **capacity to learn** to do the task
- Allow people to **make decisions** about the task
- Give people **authority** to choose how they do the task
- **Support** with coaching and mentoring
- **Give credit** for the task to the person you delegated it to
- **Track** progress without interfering

 Don't:

- Delegate the **ultimate responsibility** – that remains with you
- Expect others to complete a task **without support** from you
- Expect others to do it **exactly the same way** you would

Limiting beliefs

Beliefs are ideas we no longer question. They are the rules we make which govern our behaviour and they can drive us to success or into the ground. Once we make these subconscious rules we seek evidence in our surroundings to support them, filtering out that which does not support them.

By generalising too much, or ignoring useful information, beliefs can become limiting.

Our subconscious beliefs often surface in our conscious minds. We all have a voice inside us that tells us things. Which of these do you say to yourself?

- *'There's no point trying to manage my workload, it's just too big.'*
- *'I must achieve perfection – 100% or nothing.'*
- *'I am not good enough as I am....I must work harder.'*
- *'I have to win and they have to lose.'*
- *'I really need people to like me.'*
- *'I can't say no because.....'*
- *'I can get by with minimum effort.'*
- *'I'm best off not being organised – I please myself and I get by.'*
- *'I have to be totally organised, planned and have anticipated absolutely everything.'*

Limiting beliefs – strategies

If you identified phrases you say to yourself, what is the impact on you of believing these things? If you secretly ignored one because you didn't like it, what is it telling you?

Changing the limiting beliefs that hold you back begins with raising your awareness of the thoughts that stop you from being successful.

1. Keep a thought log over a three day period.
2. Record the thoughts you have in response to things that go well and in response to things that do not go well.
3. Analyse the thoughts and consider the underlying rules that you have about that situation.

Example:

In response to a very busy lunch time, when your planned priorities were hijacked by a serious incident in the school playground, you found yourself saying, 'it's impossible to stay organised'. The underlying rule here may be that trying to be organised is futile. The response to this may be to give up the techniques you use to organise yourself, and you then fulfil this belief.

Limiting beliefs – strategies

There are two cycles of thinking which influence us in our everyday lives:

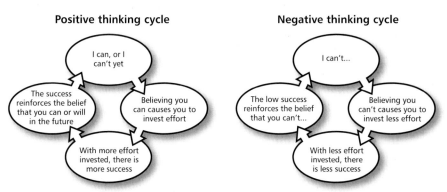

Positive thinking cycle

- I can, or I can't yet
- Believing you can causes you to invest effort
- With more effort invested, there is more success
- The success reinforces the belief that you can or will in the future

Negative thinking cycle

- I can't...
- Believing you can't causes you to invest less effort
- With less effort invested, there is less success
- The low success reinforces the belief that you can't...

Thinking positively creates the behaviours that lead to success rather than failure.

Limiting beliefs – strategies

We literally talk ourselves into or out of success. To beat the limiting beliefs we need to catch the negative thoughts and 'reframe' (change them) to more resourceful thoughts.

Reframing
Taking the negative thoughts, writing them down and then identifying positive alternatives is a technique that with practice becomes automatic. Over time you will no longer need to write the thoughts down. Here are some helpful questions to ask yourself to help you reframe:

- Now that I think about it, how could I still make something useful happen here?
- What are the opportunities in this situation?
- Where you hear yourself using words like *always, never, consistently, hopeless,* eg in relation to the behaviour of a child or year group, challenge yourself by turning the word into a question: *always? never?*
- How could I contradict this?
- Add *'yet'* to the end of any statement you hear yourself say which starts with *'I can't'*, eg *'I can't yet'*

Limiting beliefs – strategies

In the example on page 46 the new self-talk might become:

'It is important that I respond appropriately to this incident. I have sufficient skills and flexibility in my approach to my workload to find another time to complete the task I had planned for this lunchtime. So how can I still achieve this?'

This can feel a little strange, almost like lying to yourself, at first. What you are actually doing is staying in control of your situation and avoiding the rush of negative emotions which can lead you to feelings of despair.

Interaction behaviours

Essentially there are four types of interaction behaviour that we use with others:

- Passive
- Aggressive
- Assertive
- Passive-aggressive

Passive, aggressive and assertive behaviour all have their uses.
Passive-aggressive behaviour is an unhelpful pattern for ourselves and others.

Passive behaviour

The **general characteristics** of passive behaviour are:
- Compliance, resignation to fate, pleasantness, self-criticism, and pessimism

The **downside** of this behaviour is:
- Danger of being victimised, being overworked, losing self-respect, stirring anger in others, boredom, lack of fulfilment and quiet attention-seeking

The **upside** of this behaviour is:
- It is low-risk, safe, appears modest, avoids danger

Use to: melt into the background, show modesty, allow others to take the lead.

Aggressive behaviour

The **general characteristics** of aggressive behaviour are:
- Dominance, forcefulness, mistrust, criticism of others, impatience, hunger for status

The **downside** of this behaviour is:
- Can be abusive, encourages others to be aggressive, can make others feel threatened, harbours destructive emotions, can damage relationships in the long-term

The **upside** of this behaviour is:
- Allows us to express genuine anger, can work well in crisis situations, gets you noticed, can get you what you need quickly

Use to: defend yourself verbally under extreme pressure, show your anger, get noticed. (Use sparingly and be in control – it gives unpredictable results!)

Assertive behaviour

 The **general characteristics** of assertive behaviour are:
- Fairness, sensitivity, respect for others, reflection, optimism and confidence

 The **downside** of assertive behaviour is:
- It exerts limited power, you may be disliked by others for expressing your needs

 The **upside** of assertive behaviour is:
- Independence, facilitates democracy and sound relationships, enables managed risks to be taken, respects others, helps you get others to support your goals

Use to: be decisive, effectively communicate your point, handle criticism, negotiate, communicate your needs whilst respecting those of others.

When to be assertive

Assertive behaviour is a way of being clear about your needs without imposing them upon others.

Behaving assertively will not always get you what you want or need, but it will enable you to make your needs clear and stand up to others who overstep your boundaries. It's essential in managing workload that you behave assertively if you are to maintain your working envelope.

When you should be assertive

- When you are happy to reveal your thoughts and needs
- When you are looking to maintain healthy relationships
- When others are impinging on your time or your rights

Saying yes when you should say no

It can be so hard sometimes to say no to a request, particularly if it is delivered in either a very reasonable or very forceful way. You may say yes when you actually mean no.

When a request is made of you always consider:

- **Appropriateness** – is it appropriate for me to do this? Is there someone else better suited? Why does this need doing?
- **Urgent/important** – where does this task fit in the urgent/important grid? Is this something I should be taking on?
- **Working envelope** – given my working envelope, how much time will this take and how will it fit into my schedule? When is the deadline for this?

Having asked these questions of the task, you can then respond.

More about assertiveness

The next time someone makes a request that exceeds your boundaries, remember you always have at least four choices of response according to where the request fits in terms of the urgent/important grid:

1. Say yes! (if it fits into your working envelope)
2. Make a counter offer, *'I can't do that, but what I can do is....'* or, *'If I do this, it means that X won't happen until Y – how do you feel about that?'*
3. Say no assertively, or if it helps in your mind, say, *'I'm saying yes to saying no!'*
4. Defer request to collect more information/check your diary

Other useful tips:
- Pay due respect to the feelings of others: *'I appreciate that you might be angry about this, but I feel strongly that we need to do it like this...'* or, *'I'm sorry that you feel upset, and.....'*

- Repeating your point over and again is called the 'broken record technique' and is very helpful in the face of stiff opposition, *'I hear what you are saying but I can't....'*

Passive-aggressive behaviour

One of the most destructive behaviour patterns to use is the passive-aggressive loop. Passive-aggressive behaviour occurs when we aren't necessarily clear about how someone's actions affect us, but we take out the anger that their actions create in us in clandestine ways. Passive-aggressive behaviour is characterised by saying everything is OK (when it's not) and then talking angrily about the situation to others.

Example:

You are upset about the decisions taken about a new approach to gathering grades in the department. You don't express your thoughts directly but instead brood about the issue and choose a suitable mood to adopt to 'punish' others, or you respond deliberately slowly to other requests by the person at the centre of your angst. You criticise the person in the staffroom.

Passive-aggressive behaviour damages relationships, causes confusion, and doesn't actually solve the problem. It is also self-destructive as it encourages the festering of negative emotion. Everyone loses out and most of all you!

Interaction behaviours – strategies

Assertive behaviour is an excellent behaviour to develop because of its respect for others' rights, as well as your own. It allows you to make your position clear and non-negotiable if necessary.

Behaving appropriately is the recipe for managing your time effectively and there are times when a more **aggressive** or **passive** stance may be the best approach. Building your confidence in managing your time, and the demands that others make on it, is about being flexible in your approach. People who use the range of these three behaviours appropriately are confident and maintain healthy personal boundaries with others.

Avoiding the self-destructive **passive-aggressive** behavioural response prevents the escalation of unhelpful negative emotions and thoughts.

Work-Life
Balance

 Winning
Attitudes

 Great
Habits

 Taming
Time

 Looking
After Yourself

 Self-evaluation
Framework

Great
Habits

Effective planning

To plan your time effectively and achieve your goals you will need to make written plans, and to do this you will need:

- A diary
- A record of your goals for the year
- A current projects list
- A weekly planning outline (page 66)
- A daily to do list
- A wallet file to store your records of goals and action plans

Your diary

Every effective person has a way of organising their schedule. This usually centres around a paper-based or electronic diary. There are some elaborate and expensive approaches to diarising your schedule. All you need is a simple way to record and overview commitments and priorities.

It is largely a matter of personal preference as to whether you choose a:

- Standard/academic year paper diary
- Loose-leaf file diary (eg filofax™)
- Electronic palm-top device (may synchronise with PC)
- a PC-based diary

Whatever you choose it should have a week-to-a-view format and a vertical planner for the whole year. For most teachers, portability and speed of access to information is an important consideration. This may rule out the exclusive use of electronic diaries on a fixed computer.

Your diary

Setting up your diary properly involves recording in the main body of the diary
all dates and commitments including meetings, holidays, and special events.
These should be repeated in the vertical planning element of the diary for an overview.

- Get into the habit of putting commitments into the vertical planner at the same time as they go into the main body of the diary
- Use colours/highlighters to mark regular commitments in the vertical planner

'Organisation is the key to managing the workload. Especially useful was the advice given to me by my mentor. She got me to plan out the whole of the term. I am able to easily see the big picture for the whole term. I definitely aim to plan ahead carefully as much as possible throughout my teaching career. It has made a big difference.'

**David Kynes,
Student Teacher, Hull**

Using your diary

Once a deadline is upon you it's causing pressure:

- Carefully break more complex tasks down into steps, eg setting up end of term exams for Year 7. Write the steps in your diary, eg a letter to parents by date Z, needs to go to tutors by date Y, therefore needs to go to reprographics by date X, therefore needs to be written by W, therefore need information by date V

- For longer-term tasks write in a series of reminders on the days, or weeks, before the deadline

- Write in the diary in pencil – things change; you can rub them out and reschedule

Goals and priorities

Your diary is not just for recording commitments; it forms the basis for your planning as well. You will need to:

* Keep a written copy of the goals you set for the next 12 months (see page 25)
* Keep a rolling record of the key tasks/projects you are working on
* Each week, from the goals and projects, plan the priorities for the week into your schedule
* Action plan complex goals and tasks into smaller units, breaking them down and giving them interim deadlines, allocating time to work on them in your diary

It is essential, if you are to manage your workload, to know at all times the goals you are working on. Keep these items in your wallet file to help you log progress and plan to meet your goals. To help you maintain steady progress it is important to review your goals and tasks regularly. The following pages introduce a neat weekly planning grid which is simple to use and ensures that your goals are always in your mind.

Planning each week

Staying organised involves spending some time each week assessing your priorities. Twenty minutes spent identifying priorities linked to your goals for the coming week is time very well spent. Once the new week is upon you it is too late to plan it. So setting your priorities for the following week is best done within the previous week.

The grid on the following pages can be used as a support to planning. It is available as an electronic version for you to modify at **www.visionforlearning.co.uk** in the 'workload' area of the site.

Putting your year goals into the weekly planning grid (you can copy or print copies after doing this once) is a superb way of keeping your goals in mind and focusing on priorities. Identify the priorities for the week that will bring you closer to achieving your goals.

Remember this is for all of your life.

A weekly planning grid:

This year's goals	This week	Monday *To do:*	Tuesday *To do:*	Wednesday *To do:*	Thursday *To do:*	Friday *To do:*	Weekend *To do:*
		Registration	Registration	Registration	Registration	Registration	Saturday
		P1	P1	P1	P1	P1	
		P2	P2	P2	P2	P2	
		B	B	B	B	B	
		P3	P3	P3	P3	P3	
		P4	P4	P4	P4	P4	Sunday
		L	L	L	L	L	
		P5	P5	P5	P5	P5	
		P6	P6	P6	P6	P6	
		Registration	Registration	Registration	Registration	Registration	
		After school	After school	After school	After school	After school	
		Evening	Evening	Evening	Evening	Evening	

Paper copies work best printed onto A3 paper. Add your goals before printing a copy from the 'workload' area of http://visionforlearning.co.uk/mlpbresources

Planning each day

With your weekly priorities etc, you'll need to ensure that you plan each day to move towards those goals.

- Make a 'to do' list for the day. Use the urgent/important grid (page 38) to help you. Rank those priorities from 1-5. Record these in order of importance in the 'to do' section in the grid for that day. Use this to guide how you spend time that day
- If you lose some of the time you hoped for, knowing that you accomplished even one or two tasks means you have done what is most important
- Tick off the tasks when complete and congratulate yourself when a job is done

'I do not put the word 'free' on my timetable. I have allocated each slot to a particular task and I try to stick quite rigidly to that. For example, one slot a week is for timetable issues. I have a clear start and end time for my day and I stick to it. I only go into email twice a day.'

**Chris Smith,
Senior Teacher, Midlands**

Flexibility

Once you are planning each week you will start to become more aware of the flexibility you have to get the most important things done. You'll worry less about those less important issues.

The best laid plans can be hijacked by others and from time to time unforeseen issues crop up. But how much choice do you have? Always check the unexpected against your priorities.

- Must it be me who deals with this?
- Do I need to deal with it right now?
- Is it really more important than my priorities?
- Could it be dealt with later?

Whatever comes your way, keep your goals and priorities in mind.

Holiday time

Your holidays are tremendously important when you teach. Using them well allows you to recuperate and recharge your batteries so that you can perform effectively and maintain your resilience in term time. It is essential that you do this.

You should by now have a working envelope. This means that holiday is holiday.

Holiday time

If **you** decide it is **absolutely essential** to use your holiday time to work, then remember:

- Parkinson's law still applies: work will expand to fill the time you make available to it. Set a very tight boundary on the time you will spend

- Set a clear outcome in advance for the task you wish to tackle

- Ensure you take the necessary materials and information with you to do the task

- Decide what you will do if you don't finish the task in the time you allocated, eg decide when you will be able to finish it when you return to work, consider getting help with the task

- Work away from your relaxation spaces at home and take regular breaks

- Use holiday work time for getting ahead, **NOT** catching up. It is psychologically soul-destroying to use valuable holiday for catching up. Work on enhancing your work-life balance for the next half term. If catch-up is a problem now, alternate between catch-up and get-ahead tasks during the allocated holiday work time

Staying organised – a case study

Jane never felt on top of things. There was always marking to be done, lessons to plan and so many unexpected jobs others asked her to do. Regularly working a sixty hour week, she was very tired within a couple of weeks of term starting. She had mouth ulcers and lost her temper easily in class. Things had become unbearable. Jane began to look at how she was managing her time. She found:

- That the marking workload was something she could manage (see page 78)
- If she cut down the amount of time she worked each week, she could put in more things to look forward to and feel rested. She **set a working envelope** (see pages 28-32)
- She realised she would never finish everything she **could**, but she could complete everything she **had** to do in a shorter time by **prioritising** (see page 38)
- She realised that she had forgotten how to **spend time relaxing** and this in itself stopped her from stopping – a kind of subconscious **fear of stopping**
- When she was tired and irritable her students caused her more behavioural issues – **she reacted better when she was more resourceful**

Moving on

As we've seen, our attitude to our work and the boundaries we lay down influence the degree to which we achieve work-life balance.

Remember:

- Keep sight of what's important in your life
- Decide on your realistic working envelope
- Prioritise
- Plan each and every day
- Be realistic and flexible
- Say yes to saying no

With the changes you have already made from the first sections of this book you are now on track to create the work-life balance you desire. The next section details more practical strategies for using time effectively.

Work-Life
Balance

 Winning
Attitudes

 Great
Habits

 Taming
Time

 Looking
After Yourself

 Self-evaluation
Framework

Taming Time

A personal story

Cathy Groves is a highly successful and dedicated teacher:

'The most important step for me was to realise that I could still be a worthwhile person, valued colleague and good teacher without working every hour of the day and night. Once I had grasped that, it was easier to make the changes I needed to make without feeling guilty. Unfortunately, I waited until I was in a state of extreme stress before acting. Changing the way I worked then became a priority for the sake of my health, so I spoke to lots of friends and colleagues to find their top tips on managing time, and decided just how much time I would give each week to school and how much I would keep for myself.
It has worked. I am now happier, healthier and enjoying the whole of my life.'

Cathy's top tip:
Websites have a lot of good worksheets which can save you making your own.
Several times a year, get together with colleagues to share the best stuff – it saves you all time!

Tips and strategies

This section offers a host of time-taming strategies specifically gathered for the education environment. For ease of reference, think of them as categorised into the following areas:

Learning and teaching (pages 76-78)
People (pages 79-86)
Administration and environment (pages 87-96)

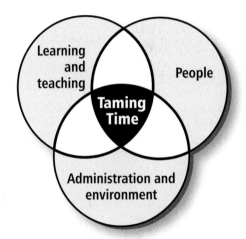

Learning and teaching

It is of great comfort to learn that minimising teacher workload in the classroom can go hand in hand with maximising student achievement.

Who is working hardest in your classroom?
You or your students? If it's you, chances are that learning isn't happening optimally. Because learning is something that is done by students, not something done to them, promoting it is more about facilitation, and less about delivery.

To get students learning we need to create climates and opportunities in class that get them actively involved and excited about learning.

Accelerated learning

Accelerated Learning (AL) is an excellent approach to enhanced learning and teaching. It has the advantage of providing insight into how our brains learn, offering practical strategies to improve learning and results, while minimising the impact of negative stress in classrooms.

It can also **reduce teacher workload** through:

- Its approaches to reducing levels of challenging behaviour, increasing motivation and improving relationships between teachers and students
- Focusing on facilitation and reducing reliance on teacher delivery
- Increased use of peer, formative assessment, which reduces the marking burden
- Greater success in building long-term memory, reducing exam pressure points

It falls outside the scope of this book to deal fully with these aspects of learning and teaching, but an excellent resource is *The Accelerated Learning Pocketbook* by Brin Best and *Accelerated Learning, A User's Guide* by Alistair Smith.

Marking and feedback

Some evidence shows children pay little attention to written feedback where a grade is given. Effective feedback encourages children to reflect and is surprisingly smart in terms of teacher workload. Consider using the following techniques more of the time:

- Set clear criteria for work – students with focus make fewer mistakes – less to correct
- Set some work as concept maps – you can get a good overview of understanding
- Use dots to indicate an error, but write nothing else – encourage reflection
- Use peer feedback which identifies a 4:1 ratio of strengths:development points
- Mark one piece of work in three, and use peer feedback for the others
- Students share their work before they submit it and correct their own mistakes
- Put marks on school intranet using anonymous coding system. This saves time reading marks out and encourages interest in getting feedback
- Speed-mark by marking a question at a time rather than a whole test paper at a time

Sorting out problems with others

Teachers often need to help resolve **disputes** and defuse **tensions** among people around them. The principles are similar for children and adults:

1. Try to choose a physical environment which is conducive to discussion.
2. Focus on listening and build rapport.
3. Where there are strong emotions like anger and frustration, let people vent them where possible.
4. Once they have vented their emotions ask them how they would prefer things to be.
5. Ask them what the situation is currently like.
6. Relay back to them what they said they wanted it to be like.
7. Ask them what they think they need to do to achieve this and what help they need from others.

This process supports people whilst maintaining a sense of **empowerment**.

Other people's problems

We are often interrupted, when we desperately need to finish something, by someone with a problem. Their problem is very important to them, but may be a lower priority to you. It can be easy to drop what you are doing and meet their needs, even though you know it will add to your workload. What do you do?

- State how much time you have available now, **or** say when you do have time to listen
- Based on what you know, place the issue in the grid on page 38 – prioritise it
- You may have an instant answer – in which case give it
- Avoid taking their problem from them and dealing with it for them – it will add to your workload
- Ask them what they have tried already to resolve it
- If time is short, ask them to come back later, but leave them with a question to start them processing their own solution, eg *'What would you prefer here?'*

Coaching and mentoring

Coaching and mentoring are fine supports to your professional development and work-life balance. If you think you might benefit from the support of a coach/mentor there are some points to consider.

Choose someone who:

- Is objective enough to be honest with you
- Models the kinds of behaviours you aspire to
- You feel comfortable with
- Has a reputation for supporting others effectively
- Preferably has had some specific training in coaching and/or mentoring
- Is willing to create time to support you

There are circumstances where a person external to the organisation can be of real benefit in providing objectivity and confidentiality. Coaching support is available from professional life coaches at affordable rates.

Coaching others

How could coaching others save me time?
Because coaching is about asking questions to enable others to understand problems and find solutions **for themselves** it can save you time on two levels:

1. You only pick up the problems you absolutely have to deal with.
2. When people are encouraged to solve their own issues, they not only **find solutions** to the issue but **they learn the process** to do it next time and can apply the approach to other similar situations.

Remember that most problems people bring do not need instant solutions even though they may make it seem like that! Ask them questions to help them understand.

For more information on coaching visit
http://visionforlearning.co.uk/category/coaching-and-nlp
www.willthomasblog.com

Parents

Dealing with parents can be a most rewarding part of the teaching role. It can also build powerful supportive relationships between learners and the school.

There are times when parents make demands of us that we feel are unreasonable or unrealistic. Whilst it is our role as teachers to provide high quality learning experiences for our students, we need to maintain a sense of manageability about what we agree to in terms of individual support.

When we feel under pressure from parents, it is a good opportunity to practise our assertiveness skills (pages 53-56).

7 steps with difficult parents

When complaints or concerns are dealt with sensitively from the start, satisfaction is maximised and time spent in resolution is minimised.

Use the seven steps to satisfaction:

1. Listen and acknowledge – **allow them to express themselves** uninterrupted.
2. Ask them what they think they need in order to resolve the issue.
3. Agree to reasonable requests. Consider when and who will action them.
4. Add any further elements to the solution you feel are necessary.
5. Give a **clear** and **realistic** date when you will contact them and tell them about progress.
6. Ask them how they are feeling now and allow any further expression – take any further action needed to reassure them.
7. Thank them and remind them you have their child's best interests at heart.

Know your support staff

Schools are full of talented support staff. Get to know the people who can help you. Find out:

- Their hours
- Who else they support
- What they can and can't do
- How much notice they require for tasks

Don't stretch them too far and they will do the odd favour! Always be aware of their workload. And remember, when they do something for you, you are delegating, so use the delegation tips in this book.

Managing interruptions

Interruptions come from all sorts of places: bosses, students, parents, telephone, colleagues, even you, going off at tangents. Deal with them by:

- Asking the question: *'Is this interruption more or less important than what I'm doing at the moment?'* If it's less important than your current priority, say that you don't have time now, and give them a better time to come

- Keep interruptions short and sweet – *What do you want? Why is it needed? By when do you need it?*

- Tell people how much time you have for them – stick to that time

- Break rapport towards the end of the time by gathering papers, looking at your watch or standing up/moving

- Find a place to go in school where people are less likely to find you!

Telephone calls

The telephone is an invaluable tool in school for communication. Here are some simple tips to get it working **for you** not against you:

- Save time, be clear: identify yourself and your role, write notes
- Be ready when making calls to leave a brief answer-phone message
- Create a space in your day that is a good time to receive calls so you can let people know when you are available – saves telephone ping-pong!
- At the start of the call, tell the person on the other end of the phone how much time you have – stick to that time
- If you are making the call, have all relevant information available
- When returning a call, don't feel obliged to keep retrying – if they want you they'll call you back
- Give out your mobile number sparingly
- At home, screen calls with your answer-phone to hang on to your time

Paperwork and e-work

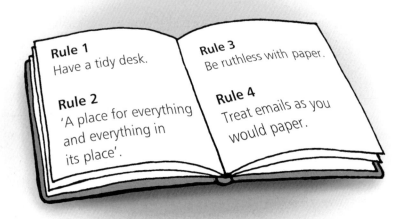

Rule 1
Have a tidy desk.

Rule 2
'A place for everything
and everything in
its place'.

Rule 3
Be ruthless with paper.

Rule 4
Treat emails as you
would paper.

Rule 1 – a tidy desk

Whether you have an office, a classroom, or a work area elsewhere, you need to keep your primary working area clear.

OK, this is it – the moment you have been waiting for.......right now: sit at your desk and clear absolutely everything off the surface! Put it on chairs or the floor and look at the empty space ahead of you. Place your diary and planning file in the centre and a pen.

From now on this is how your desk is going to stay...

You now have a primary working area which you will be keeping clear. This is a place for processing tasks not dumping things.

❝ *Clear desk....clear mind* ❞

Rule 2 – 'a place for everything...'

Now you need to sort out the stuff you've removed and give it a place.
Set up a filing system to make storing and retrieving papers easy.

You will need:
- A filing cabinet or several cardboard boxes
- Additional cardboard
- The top of a copier paper box or similar
- A black felt tip pen

'I keep my long-term reference material stored in a filing cabinet, short-term materials and issues being worked on in clip folders in a cupboard for easy access and updating. I also keep a constantly updated list of all the 'balls that are up in the air' and a 'to do' list. If it is on the list, I am dealing with it and there should be no surprises!'

**Donat Morgan,
Oakley College**

Rule 2 – 'a place for everything…'

If you don't have a space to work in school, then it is a priority for you to find one. In this space you will need to make sure you have a clear and organised workspace:

1. List every aspect of your role in school, eg teaching, marking, report writing, pastoral, Duke of Edinburgh's Award, etc. Add 'miscellaneous' to the list.
2. This list is your filing system. Alphabetise it. Putting it in a spreadsheet will allow you to alphabetise quickly.
3. Set up folders using your list. Store in a filing cabinet, or use cardboard boxes as an alternative, with spare card as dividers.
4. Set up the same filing system in your computer workspace using the folders function. Repeat again in your email area.

> **Now you file and retrieve using the same system everywhere.**

Rule 3 – be ruthless with paper

Now that you have a filing system it's time to use it.
Handle paper once.

Work through the pile of materials from your
desk and categorise under one of three
headings:

Action: Deal with it now

File: Genuine reference material and
jobs you will need to come back
to later (decide which role it
fits and put it in the filing
cabinet/box – record jobs for
later in your diary)

Bin: If it is not for action and is not a
key document to refer to, put it
in the bin!

Rule 4 – treat emails as you would paper

❝ Handle e-work once. ❞

- Set up files in your inbox and in your 'My Documents' folder which match your paper filing system. You can create subfolders also if this helps you. In this way you can file emails and attachments in the same system as your paperwork. It makes retrieval and storage so much easier

- Delete unsolicited mail immediately, without reading it

- If you need to send an email internally which is more complex than 20 lines of text, speak to the person instead

'Email is a godsend, but can become habit-forming. Switch off the prompt that tells you you have new email. It is a two-way process: the more you send the more replies you will get – use it sparingly.'
Dee Gilmour, Design Teacher

The result

At the end of this process you will have:

- The contents of your working area filed in an easily retrievable system
- A list of the actions you must take and by when
- A waste-paper bin full of lots of things that are out of date
- A PC hard-drive and email which are easy to use
- A nice clear desk to operate from

Now, take a break and celebrate your steps towards work-life balance

And finally……

- Get into the habit of dealing with your staffroom tray in the same way as things on your desk – action it, file it, bin it
- File papers each day and week as you get them
- Keep a slim wallet file for the week of this week's immediate paperwork….BUT….always review and file it at the end of the week

The learning workspace

Maximising the use of your classroom workspace for carrying out the teaching role is of prime importance in managing workload.

If you have your own classroom, organise the space:

- Have a cupboard which locks for the things you need each lesson
- Label cupboards clearly so you and your students know the contents
- Keep your desk tidy by having a place for everything
- Operate a system for filing paperwork in the classroom
- Have systems in place to store and check resources so they remain intact

The nomadic teacher

When you don't have your own classroom and move around a lot there are particular challenges.

Some tips to help:

- Get to know all of the rooms you will teach in before you take a class there
- Identify a storage place for books and resources in each room
- Buy a plastic compartmentalised box for common resources
- Wherever possible use a wheeled bag to move your resources and protect your back
- Explore who can help you to move resources
- Always have your own chalk/board markers and a board rubber in your bag
- Take 30 seconds at the start of each lesson to collect your thoughts
- Use the marking tips in this section to maximise in-class feedback and minimise moving exercise books

Work-Life
Balance

 Winning
Attitudes

 Great
Habits

 Taming
Time

 Looking
After Yourself

 Self-evaluation
Framework

Looking After
Yourself

Pressure and stress

This section explores the nature and effects of stress and looks at ways to reduce it. By taking control, setting goals and staying organised you will have already reduced your stress levels.

Pressure can be created by:

- Deadlines and targets
- Problems
- Mistakes made by you and others
- Challenges
- People
- Sheer weight of work
- Uncertainties in your role
- Self-limiting beliefs

Stress is the response **you** have to the pressures you face.

Stress hormones

When the stress hormones cortisol and adrenaline race around in your blood they trigger a variety of preparations for emergencies, including the four F's (Smith A. 1999)

FIGHT: Aggressively standing your ground, physically or verbally

FLIGHT: Moving away from, or diverting attention from, the threat

FLOCK: Banding together with others – safety in numbers

FREEZE: Physically or mentally frozen and unable to think or act

At lower levels of secretion the hormones improve concentration and readiness for learning. At higher levels they inhibit learning, interfere with the laying down of long-term memory and cause potentially life-threatening conditions.

The mechanism of stress

Another way of looking at it is that stress comes in two colours:

Green stress is the stuff of peak performance.
- Gets you out of bed
- Energises you
- Stimulates creativity
- Gives you a keen edge
- Heightens performance

Red stress is the stuff of crisis, of emergency and of short-term solutions

- Erodes your ability to think
- Affects your memory
- Can lead to health-related problems
- Stimulates unhelpful behaviours
- Limits performance

The colour of stress you experience depends largely on your outlook and how you manage the pressure that comes your way.

Healthy body, healthy mind

Looking after your body and your mind are vital aspects to managing your workload.

An unhealthy body and mind lead to poor energy levels, low motivation and negative thinking patterns and emotions. This in turn leads to low levels of resilience and makes it hard to maintain the kinds of positive behaviours we have explored in this book.

In the longer term not looking after your health can lead to physical and mental illness.

Maintaining resilience

We have an internal **resilience** bank account. When we continue to draw on our resilience bank account without putting anything back in, our account becomes **overdrawn**. This overdraft leads to stress, reduced performance, negative emotions, damaged relationships, and eventually ill health. Over a long period it can shorten your life.

There are inevitably times of unexpected demand in your role. These will draw on your reserves and can actually be exciting. However, if you have few reserves within you, then you will begin to experience all demands as negative **stress**.

Maintaining resilience

How to minimise stress:

- **Plan ahead** for the long-, medium- and short-term
- Block out planning and relaxation time each week and take it
- Be **realistic** with your plans
- Be **flexible** towards your plans and build in enough **margin** for coping with unexpected demands – a teacher will always have them!
- Make **lists** and **tick off** things you achieve – praise yourself
- Take **time out** during the day – even a few seconds without stimulus can help psychologically
- Eat and drink **healthily**, especially water (eight glasses per day)
- Create time for **exercise** and **mental space**
- Do something for **YOU** each week, something you enjoy and look forward to
- As a teacher, **manage your stress** because it **affects your students** too
- Seek **help** from others if you feel you are suffering from too much stress

Your long-term health

Poor work-life balance has short-term effects on our ability to achieve deadlines, sustain relationships, and memorise. Long-term it can have real consequences for our health. An array of diseases is caused or intensified by stress, including cardio vascular disease, immune problems, panic attacks and depression, ulcers, colitis.

There is a prescription that starts us in the right direction to short- and long-term health...it is....... R. E. S. T. which stands for:

Refuel – eat and drink properly for maximum performance
Exercise – take regular exercise for posture, health and stamina
Stop – take stimulus-free time
Time to reflect on your successes and plan your next steps to aid work-life balance

Refuel

We hear a great deal in the news about obesity and poor diet. The figures suggest a nation eating inappropriately. A balanced diet of unprocessed foods with plenty of fruit and vegetables is at the heart of good health.

There is strong evidence now to link poor diet with life-threatening diseases like cancer and cardiovascular disease. It is well known that we need a balanced diet for long-term health. We now also know that what we eat and drink affects our mental as well as our physical well-being in more immediate ways.

Refuel: lousy eating – lousy feelings

Teachers' fix

Caffeinated drinks, eg coffee, coke and tea, cause our nerves to misfire and create alertness hyper-states. This affects sleep, creates irregular heart rates and feelings of anxiety. Cut back for a couple of weeks and notice the benefits. Drink water instead.

Teachers' famine

Going for long periods during the day without food leads the body to think it is facing famine. We develop low blood sugar levels leading to headaches, irritability and feeling low in energy. This can promote the deposition of fat when we next eat. Set some boundaries about eating well in school and stick to them and eat away from your desk!

Refuel: lousy eating – lousy feelings

Teachers' rush
Eating high carbohydrate foods like chocolate and
bread create high sugar loads in the
bloodstream in very short time frames.
The body responds with high insulin release
and over-zealous blood sugar reduction.
A lack of energy follows the initial rush.
We can feel extremely tired after sugary
foods and irritability and poor
concentration follow. Avoid
sugary foods like
chocolate and replace
with slow-release
carbohydrates balanced
with fat and protein.

Refuel

Water

Water makes up 80% of the body and surrounds every cell. Our cells carry out all of the specialised functions in our body. Many work together to balance our internal chemistry.

Cells suffer when there is insufficient water around. You've only to think back to your last hangover to know the physical symptoms of dehydration:

- Cell energy production is compromised and headaches occur
- Brain cells are sensitive to dehydration and learning is impaired
- One of the early signs of dehydration is irritability
- Prolonged low water levels in the body can compromise kidney function

When you are well hydrated, you feel great!
Get into the habit of drinking water during the day and remember that caffeine exacerbates water loss. The more caffeine you take, the more water you need to drink.

Exercise

Even moderate exercise is good for you. The British Heart Foundation (www.bhf.org.uk) recommends five sessions of exercise per week each lasting around 30 minutes. Exercise should raise your heart rate and breathing rate and make you feel a little warm.

Here's why building in exercise is so beneficial:

- Boosts feel-good chemical levels – endorphins and enkephalins
- Enhances concentration and alertness
- Encourages healthy functioning of cardiovascular system
- Improves muscle and lung performance
- Supports healthier weight
- Helps you look and feel better, enhancing self-esteem

Over two thirds of us do less than the recommended amount of physical activity!

Exercise

Where are you now?

EXERCISE PATTERN CURRENTLY	✔
I never exercise	
I am considering beginning to exercise	
I occasionally exercise	
I exercise regularly and have done so over the last six months	

What is your next step?

Exercise

You don't have to go to a gym!

Choose an exercise you will enjoy.
One of the finest exercises is walking.

How could you bring more exercise into your day?

Case study
Tony did no exercise at all. He felt that his day was long enough at school without adding a further half hour of exercise. When he got home in the evening he was exhausted and never felt like it. He decided to try walking and built up to a 30 minute walk each morning for 5 days of the week. Now he wouldn't be without his walk, whatever the weather. He says that some of his best ideas come while he walks and what's more he feels full of energy all day and well into the evening. He says, **'I have a little bit of space for myself each day – it's great.'**

Stop

In the 21st century we have forgotten the meaning of stop.

We have truly forgotten how to rest and provide ourselves with a low stimulus environment. Teachers may have in excess of 70 human interactions per hour in a typical day. That could mean as many as 500 interactions in one day!

When you finish your day make time to reduce the number of stimuli.

Ideas:

- Meditate and clear your mind through focusing on your breathing
- Sit quietly and read the paper
- Close your eyes and think of being in your dream location
- Spend some time with someone you care about
- Spend some time with a pet
- Take a walk or some other form of gentle exercise

Stop

Sleep

We averagely need 7-8 hours sleep per night. Without this our ability to function in the day is impaired.

An alarming number of the workforce suffer from varying degrees of insomnia. You can improve your sleep by:

- Avoiding caffeinated drinks for four hours before bedtime
- Eating regularly during the day
- Relaxing for at least an hour before you retire to bed
- Making sure your bed is comfortable and the room is adequately ventilated and heated
- Considering meditation techniques if you have difficulty clearing your mind before bed
- Taking steps throughout your life to minimise stress

Stop

Promoting health and well-being

There are dozens of complementary and alternative approaches to promoting health and well-being which treat the body holistically.

These include:

- Aromatherapy
- Massage
- Reflexology
- Reiki
- Acupuncture

There are a number of centres across the country that focus specifically on preventative approaches to managing stress and promoting well-being.

Consider regular well-being maintenance through complementary approaches.

Take stock

Reflecting on progress is important in terms of improving how to approach tasks and situations in the future. It is also vital to review and celebrate your successes.

Ring-fenced reflection
1. Switch off the part of you that considers what didn't go so well.
2. Reflect on and list all the successes – big and small – this week, term, year.
3. For each success identify the strengths you showed in achieving that success.
4. Take some time to reflect on your success and congratulate yourself.
5. File these and bring them out again when the going gets tough.

Wider reflection
1. Consider what things did not go well.
2. What would make them run more smoothly in future?
3. What did you learn about yourself in this situation?
4. How does this new knowledge help you in the future?
5. Set a specific goal for improvement and add to your list of goals.

Take stock

Feed your spirit

In times of high pressure we can forget to look after our spiritual self. Build in time to do something that brings you a sense of escape and connects you spiritually.

Learn a new skill, do something different or read something that feeds your spirit. There are some excellent books which can help to keep you in touch with yourself and beyond.

Five great books to calm the mind and feed the spirit:

Stillness Speaks by Eckhart Tolle

The Alchemist by Paulo Coehlo

The Celestine Prophecy by James Redfield

THE ROAD LESS TRAVELLED BY M. SCOTT PECK

Jonathan Livingston Seagull by Richard Bach

Five great books to calm the mind and feed the spirit

Work-Life Balance

Winning Attitudes

Great Habits

Taming Time

Looking After Yourself

Self-evaluation Framework ◀

Self-evaluation Framework

Self-evaluation Framework

The self-evaluation framework on the following pages helps you to take a closer, more analytical look at your workload management. Follow the steps below:

1. Read the questions and **score** yourself as indicated:
   0 = you feel you have not begun to address the question
   1 = you have started work, but it is in its early stages
   2 = you feel quite confident about the work you have done in this area
   3 = you feel the work you have done in this area represents excellent practice

2. As you go, note down any **action points** or issues that come to mind – these form the basis of your action plan for improving your workload management.

3. **Add up** the scores for each section and for the whole. This will give you a more **quantitative** assessment of which areas need further development.

4. **Photocopy** the framework so you can refer back to it in future. Repeat the exercise quarterly to track your progress and identify the steps to maintain or improve.

5. Formulate your **action plan** for improving your practice, including timescales.

Work-life balance

Work-life balance	Emerging 0	1	Advanced 2	3
How clear is your work-life vision for the next year?				
Do you regularly review your work-life balance, for example at least once every three months?				
Do you reflect *honestly* on the information around you, about your work-life balance?				
Do you seek feedback from those around you at home and work, about *their* view of your work-life balance?				
Do you have a set of SMART goals for each sector of your life for the next 12 months?				
Have you set a working envelope?				
Over last month did you work within your working envelope?				

Work-life balance: [/21] = [%]

Winning attitudes

Winning attitudes	<div>◁ **Emerging**</div>0	1	<div>**Advanced** ▷</div>2	3
Do you prioritise using the URGENT-IMPORTANT grid? (page 38)				
Do you link prioritisation to your goals for the year on a weekly and daily basis?				
How aware are you of avoiding procrastination?				
If you are procrastinating, are you taking steps to combat this? (pages 40-41)				
Are you delegating everything you could?				
Are you dealing with limiting beliefs that are holding back progress?				
Are you using assertive behaviour to make clear your needs?				
Are you using passive and aggressive behaviours appropriately? (pages 51-52)				
Are you avoiding passive-aggressive behaviour? (page 57)				

Winning attitudes: ☐ /27 = ☐ %

Great habits

Great habits	◁ Emerging		Advanced ▷	
	0	1	2	3
Do you have a diary, a record of your 12-month goals, and a current projects list in use?				
Are you taking time to plan each week using the weekly planning outline or an alternative?				
Are you forming a prioritised task list for each day?				
Are you recording fixed commitments in your main diary pages and in the vertical planner?				
Are you breaking complex tasks/projects into smaller ones with your own deadlines for completion of each chunk?				
Are you ready to be flexible each day and let go of frustrations?				
Are you being careful to preserve your holiday time and focus on getting ahead?				
Do you say no when you should?				

Great habits: [/24] = [%]

Taming time

Taming time	< Emerging		Advanced ▷	
	0	1	2	3
Is the balancing of your students working and you working in class about right?				
Do you ensure learners are actively engaged in class, freeing you to support /give feedback?				
Do you use marking approaches which encourage student responsibility for progress?				
Do you look ahead to busy points, eg exam marking / report writing to minimise workload further at that time?				
Do you coach others to their own solutions?				
Do you effectively deal with interruptions?				
Do you effectively use an ordered filing system?				
Is your desk a tidy place to work?				
Do you handle paper and email once?				
Do you have an ordered teaching workspace or system for nomadic working?				

Taming time: ☐ /30 = ☐ %

Looking after yourself

Looking after yourself	◁ Emerging 0	1	Advanced ▷ 2	3
Do you manage your own stress each day?				
Are you aware of the impact of prolonged negative stress on your health?				
Are you doing something pleasurable specifically for *you* each week?				
Are you cutting back on caffeinated drinks?				
Do you take time out to eat regularly in the day?				
Are you limiting your intake of high-energy sugary foods and balancing your diet?				
Do you drink water regularly during the day?				
Are you exercising regularly?				
Do you reflect daily on your successes?				
Do you take time daily to fully *stop* and *relax*?				
Do you recognise when you have done enough?				

Looking after yourself: [/33] = [%]

Interpretation

Look at the percentages you have for each section.
Calculate your overall percentage with this formula:

$$\frac{\text{Total of raw scores for all sections:}}{135} \quad \times \quad \boxed{100} \quad = \quad \boxed{\qquad \%}$$

Date evaluation
was carried out: $\boxed{\qquad / \qquad / \qquad}$

You can use the key below to interpret the individual sections of the questionnaire as well as the overall result for your workload management.

KEY
0-29%   Emerging workload management
30-59% Improving workload management
60-89% Effective workload management
90%+   Advanced workload management

Repeating the questionnaire quarterly will enable you to track your progress.

Further Information

Websites:

Vision for Learning Ltd – www.visionforlearning.co.uk Training courses in managing workload, personal retreats, and individual coaching and hypnotherapy

www.willthomasblog.com a blog written by the author of this book, on coaching, well-being and writing. Packed with useful articles about getting your life balanced and your goals aligned with what's important to you.

Books:

The Accelerated Learning Pocketbook
by Brin Best
Published by Teachers' Pocketbooks (2003)

The Head of Department's Pocketbook
by Brin Best and Will Thomas
Published by Teachers' Pocketbooks (2003)

The Coaching and Reflecting Pocketbook
by Peter Hook, Ian McPhail & Andy Vass
Published by Teachers' Pocketbooks (2006)

Coaching Solutions. Practical Ways to Improve Performance in Schools
by W. Thomas and A. Smith
Published by Network Educational Press (2004)

The Coaching Solutions Resource Book
by W. Thomas
Published by Network Educational Press (2005)

Further Information

**Books to feed your spirit
(see page 116):**

Jonathan Livingston Seagull
by Richard Bach
Published by Avon Books

The Alchemist
by Paulo Coehlo
Published by Harper Collins

The Road Less Travelled
by M. Scott Peck
Published by Touchstone

The Celestine Prophecy
by James Redfield
Published by Warner Books

Stillness Speaks
by Eckhart Tolle
Published by Hodder Mobius

Acknowledgements

Thanks Phil, for modelling the answer to the question, *'How can I make this easier and still do it right?'* so perfectly. Thanks also to Brin Best for permission to use material from the *Head of Department's Pocketbook* and for his continuing encouragement.

My sincere thanks to Mandi Davis, Donat Morgan, David Kynes, Cathy Groves, Chris Smith, Jen, Jane, and Tony for their direct contributions to the book; to Tom Hill and Richard Vakis for their unofficial editorial support; to Linda Edge for her highly constructive and expert editorial support.

And, as always, my thanks to Mum, Dad, Sal, and Richard for their encouragement and support, now and in the darker years before work-life balance.

This book is dedicated to Jenny and Ralph.

About the author

Will Thomas BSc (Hons), MA, PGCE led a highly successful science faculty at South Bromsgrove Community College. The award-winning and best-selling author of 10 books in the field of coaching, well-being and creativity, Will is an inspirational trainer and writer in the field of human improvement. He has worked as an LA advisor and as consultant to Alistair Smith's company Alite. He is a Master Practitioner of NLP, a registered hypnotherapist and an accredited life coach. He runs Vision for Learning, an organisation that provides highly interactive and practical courses and offers coaching to support busy teaching professionals. Will is passionate about learning and making a difference in schools and colleges. He can be contacted at: www.visionforlearning.co.uk info@visionforlearning.co.uk or on 01684 892066

Courses in managing workload and personal development retreats run throughout the year. Sign up for a newsletter to hear about up coming events on the homepage at www.visionforlearning.co.uk

(www.visionforlearning.co.uk) (www.willthomasblog.com)

Order Form

Your details

Name _____

Position _____

School _____

Address _____

_____

_____

Telephone _____

Fax _____

E-mail _____

VAT No. (EC only) _____

Your Order Ref _____

Please send me:

		No. copies
Managing Workload	Pocketbook	☐
_____	Pocketbook	☐
_____	Pocketbook	☐
_____	Pocketbook	☐
_____	Pocketbook	☐

Order by Post

**Teachers'
Pocketbooks**

Laurel House, Station Approach
Alresford, Hants. SO24 9JH UK

Order by Phone, Fax or Internet

Telephone: +44 (0)1962 735573
Facsimile: +44 (0)1962 733637
E-mail: sales@teacherspocketbooks.co.uk
Web: www.teacherspocketbooks.co.uk